WHAT'S WRONG ?

THE FLETCHER FAMILY'S
PICNIC
PUZZLE

by Martin Oliver
Illustrated by Nick Abadzis

BARRON'S

It was the first day of the summer holidays – perfect weather for a picnic. Mom hummed happily for a few moments until she realized something was wrong. The house was far too quiet.

Can you help Mom find her family?

Belle wants to play with the identical triplets from next door. Can you find them?

The family gathered in the kitchen. Mom gave everyone different jobs to do – Dad was in charge of the plates, bowls, and cups, while Mom cut the bread.

Sam raided the refrigerator, Belle found the snacks, and Ella made sandwiches.

Mom made some milkshakes and at last it seemed as if they were ready to go—until Mom spotted something.

Can you see what's wrong?

Dad is trying to find his matching bicycle helmet and gloves. Can you help him?

While Dad packed the picnic things in his trailer, Mom went into the garage to get her bike. She and Dad have identical bikes but today something was wrong with hers.

Can you find the missing parts of Mom's bike?

Sam's planning to fill the wading pool but who do **you** think's going to get a surprise?

At last Mom's bike was back together. She led the way as the family cycled down the street. They were almost past the shops when Mom suddenly stopped. She had forgotten one vital ingredient for the picnic.

Mom was about to buy the first cake she saw until she remembered that everyone liked different things.

Which cake will everyone like?

Hmmm—now, if I remember rightly, Dad doesn't touch square cakes, Ella won't eat pink ones, Baby Belle only eats cakes with faces on them, and Sam doesn't like green cakes...

Can you see what Dad is buying to take on the picnic?

The cake was carefully packed away, and they all set off again.

Dad knew the way and he took the lead. He pedaled quickly and soon the shops were left behind.

He whizzed downhill and past the park. Ahead was a crossroads. Dad stopped for a second to look for the sign to the picnic area, then waved for everyone to follow him.

He had already set off down a narrow lane
when Mom checked the signpost and frowned.

Can you see what's wrong?
Which way should they go?

CASTLE
MAIN ROAD
FOREST
LAKE
TOWN CENTER
PICNIC AREA

There are four other
bike riders on this page.
Can you spot them?

Soon they were back on the right track. They rode alongside a stream, then turned a corner and stopped by a watermill. A crowd was waiting to see the mill at work, but nothing was happening.

"What's wrong, Mom?" they all asked.

The mill owner told Mom that he'd lost the key that unlocked the mill's water wheel.

Can you help him find it?

Well, I know that I put it on a brand new keyring. I remember that it had a yellow triangle label with green and pink spots on it.

Someone has lost
their two pet mice.
Can you help find them?

Everyone watched as the water wheel splashed round and round in the stream. After a while, Dad pointed to his watch—it was time to go.

Sam and Baby Belle were strapped into their seats and they all pedaled along beside a river, waving to the boats as they passed. Mom pointed at a bridge ahead and said it could be raised to let boats pass underneath.

They waited to watch a boat going under the bridge, but Mom suddenly realized that something was wrong —the bridge wasn't going up! Mom tried to raise it herself, but she didn't know which way to turn the handle.

Which way should the handle be turned to raise the bridge?

There are three fishermen by the river. Can you see what each of them has caught?

15

The captain was so grateful that Mom had raised the bridge in time that he offered the whole family a ride on his boat.

Ella was allowed to take the helm while everyone else relaxed on deck.

Baby Belle and Sam explored the boat as it chugged through the water.

At last it was time to get on with the picnic. Everything was carried off the boat and the Fletchers were about to wave goodbye when Mom suddenly stopped.

"What's wrong?" Ella asked.

Can you see what the Fletchers have left behind on the boat?

They've also moved three things belonging to the captain. Can you help him find them again?

The Fletchers pedaled on into the countryside, past a farmyard full of animals. Dad started to slow down. He got off his bike, climbed over a fence, and began unpacking the picnic.

"I've found it!" he said. "The perfect place for our picnic." But Mom wasn't so sure.

Can you see why it might not be such a good picnic spot?

The farmer's sheep have escaped. Can you help find them all?

Mom soon found a great place for the picnic. She sent the others off to explore an activity trail so she could unpack things in peace.

"That should keep them out of trouble," Mom thought. But suddenly she realized that she was wrong.

Can you see why? What is the quickest route Mom can take to take care of the problem?

Ella really likes
the activity trail.
Can you see why?

Dad kept saying that he could get down on his own, but after a few tries he was even more tangled up in the rope. Mom took charge, and slowly, Dad was untangled and gently lowered back onto solid ground.

Mom had done a great job in setting up the picnic. Ella couldn't wait to try her sandwiches, while Dad was anxious to start up his old record player.

Everything seemed to be perfect. But Sam and Baby Belle weren't happy. They wanted their matching bowls, plates, and spoons.

Can you help find them?

Dad has lost the records he wanted to play.
Can you see where they are?

Everyone piled their plates high with food.

"This is delicious," beamed Dad between mouthfuls, but Mom didn't seem very happy.

"What's wrong, Mom?" Ella asked.

"We've brought too much food," Mom said. "We'll never eat all of this."

"Don't worry," replied Dad, with a huge grin. "I think we can solve that problem—we've invited some of our friends along."

Do you recognize any familiar faces?

Toby's spotted some of his friends, too. Which of his doggy chums do you recognize?

Everyone agreed that the picnic was a great success.

"It's terrific," said Dad. "And so relaxing—
we must do it again!"

Mom gulped and turned white. Ella asked her,
"What's wrong, Mom?"

What do you think her answer was?

The answers

You'll find all the answers to the puzzles on these pages. Have a look at the "**Did you also see**" sections for lots more funny things to spot in the book.

Pages 2-3

We've circled the missing members of the family and the triplets in the picture on the right.

Ella

Triplet 1

Did you also see. . ?

A girl holding a teddy bear
A boy juggling bicycle parts

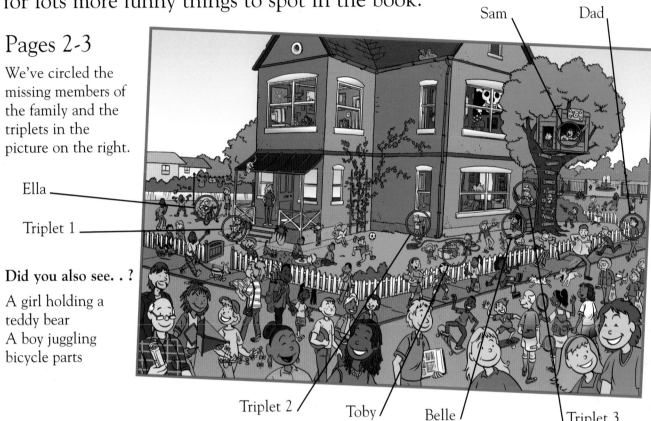

Sam   Dad

Triplet 2   Toby   Belle   Triplet 3

Page 5

Mom has spotted the cat stealing the milkshakes from the picnic basket!

Glove

Dad's matching helmet and gloves have been circled in this picture.

Glove

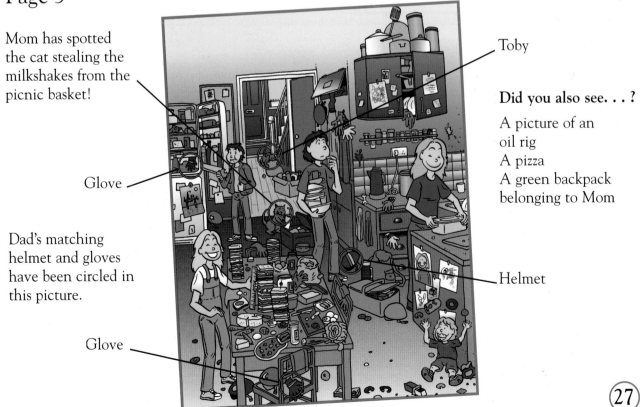

Toby

Did you also see. . . ?

A picture of an oil rig
A pizza
A green backpack belonging to Mom

Helmet

Pages 6-7

We've circled the missing parts of Mom's bike in the picture below.

Did you also see. . . ?

A family of four squirrels
A baseball bat
A red toy truck

This cat is going to get a soaking from Sam.

Kiddie Seat

Wheel

Bicycle Seat

Toby

Bell

Handlebars

Pages 8-9

Did you also see. . . ?

A ship's anchor
A shining suit of armor
A toy space rocket

Dad is buying an old-fashioned record player to take on the picnic.

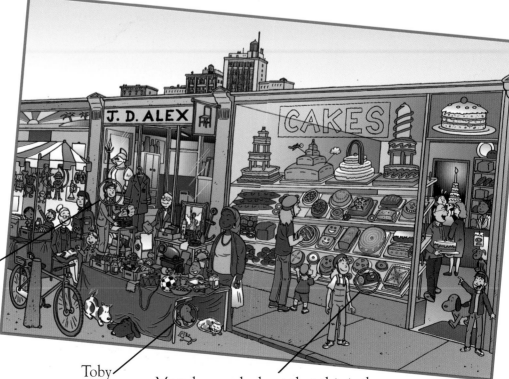

J. D. ALEX

CAKES

Toby

Mom has worked out that this is the only cake everyone will like.

Page 11

The signpost has been moved so that it is pointing in the wrong direction.
The route they should be taking is marked by the red arrow.

Did you also see. . . ?

A man tripping over a log
A camper cooking a meal
A hot-air balloon

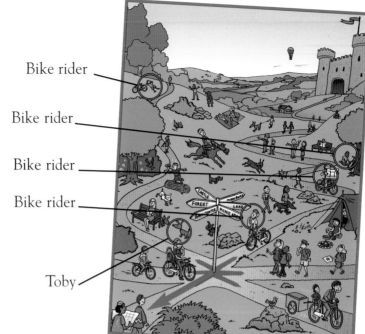

Bike rider

Bike rider

Bike rider

Bike rider

Toby

Pages 12-13

The key to unlock the water wheel is here.

Did you also see. . . ?

A baby being fed milk from a bottle
An old woman feeding the ducks
An alien!

Mouse 1

Mouse 2

Toby

Page 15

Look at the arrows on the picture to see how the cogs and pulleys work.

Mom should turn the handle clockwise to raise the bridge.

Did you also see. . . ?

A lost bike rider from page 11

Fisherman A has caught the tire.

Fisherman B has caught Fisherman C.

Fisherman C has caught the buoy.

Toby

Pages 16-17

The Fletchers have left behind five items on the boat—a backpack, a bicycle pump, a bottle of pop, a blanket, and a teddy bear. We've circled these items.

The three items belonging to the captain are in squares.

Did you also see. . . ?

The captain's cat
A treasure map
A ship in a bottle

Toby

Pages 18-19

Did you also see. . . ?

A tractor
A dog being chased by a sheep

There are 30 sheep in all.
They have been circled.

There is a fierce-looking bull near where Dad wants to have the picnic!

Toby

Toby

Pages 20-21

Dad has got tangled up in the rope swing and can't get down! The quickest route Mom can take to rescue him is marked by the dotted red line.

Did you also see. . . ?

A monkey
A shark
A fish

Ella likes the activity trail because she can use bits of the wood to make a go-kart.

Pages 22-23

We've circled Sam and Baby Belle's matching bowls, plates, and spoons in this picture.

Did you also see. . . ?

A teddy bear
A toy tricycle
The cake that Mom bought at the shop

Dad's records are in squares.

Pages 24-25

We've circled all the familiar faces.

The captain of the boat and his pet cat.

Toby

The dog from the farmyard on page 18.

The sheep shearer from page 18.

One of the bike riders from page 11.

The skateboard kids from page 3.

One of the farmer's sheep from pages 18-19.

The boy from outside the shops on page 8.

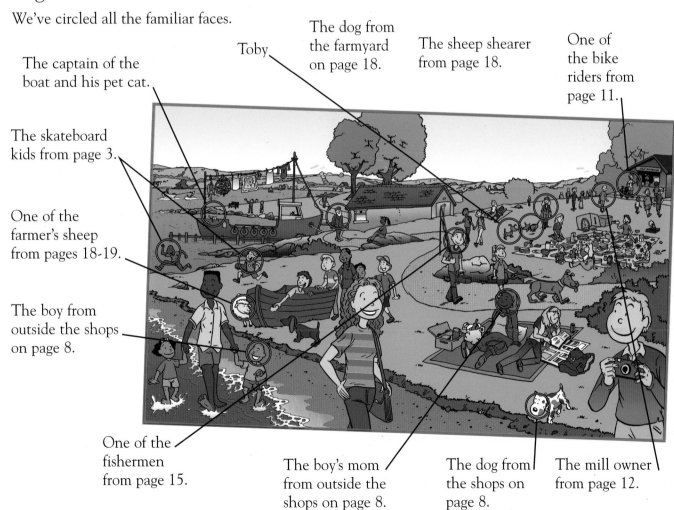

One of the fishermen from page 15.

The boy's mom from outside the shops on page 8.

The dog from the shops on page 8.

The mill owner from page 12.

Page 26

Organizing the picnic wasn't so relaxing for Mom. She is looking worried at the thought of having to do it all again!

Did you also see. . . ?

A sheep licking a cake
The fisherman hooking
a pizza

Toby

First edition for the United States, its territories and dependencies, Canada, and the Philippines published by Barron's Educational Series, Inc., 1999.

© Copyright 1999 by Martin Oliver. First published in the UK by Franklin Watts, London.

Text by Martin Oliver
Illustrations by Nick Abadzis

All inquiries should be addressed to:
Barron's Educational Series, Inc.
250 Wireless Boulevard
Hauppauge, NY 11788
http://www.barronseduc.com

ISBN 0-7641-0905-7
Library of Congress Catalog
Card Number 98-073637
Printed in Dubai
9 8 7 6 5 4 3 2 1